INTRODUCTION TO VAMPIRES

Dracula, Nosferatu, Lestat, Angel, Edward... Vampires are some of the most enduring creatures in popular culture (and not just because they live forever). They are so popular that the King of Vampires himself, Count Dracula, is one of the most featured fictional characters in movies – he makes his appearance in over 200 films and counting. Every generation seems to have its defining vampire superstar, but never before have the undead been so hot as right now.

These aren't the menacing, evil villains of ghost stories whispered in the dark – our vampires are romantic leading men, although with a definite edge! The ultimate bad boys, they have charm, they fall in love and they hate having to drink human blood to survive. Of course, they are also wildly passionate, impossibly strong and will rip the throat from anyone who tries to harm their loved ones. And it doesn't hurt that all of them just happen to be drop-dead gorgeous, too.

Scoring the role in a hot new vampire series means instant stardom for the lucky chosen actor. None of the three main men in this book – Robert Pattinson, Stephen Moyer and Ian Somerhalder – were mega-famous before they played bloodsuckers. Now they're the hottest commodities ever, and the appetite for vampires doesn't seem to be dying down anytime soon.

So, come take a walk on the dark side and sink your teeth into... *Vampire Files*!

Before you read on, it's time to take our special quiz to find out who would be your ideal bloodsucking companion...

WHO IS YOUR PERFECT VAMPIRE BOYFRIEND?

1. You would be attracted to a vampire because...
a) He is extraordinarily beautiful and you can't take your eyes off him.
b) He glamours you into thinking he's irresistible.
c) He is mysterious and could be described as being an 'old soul'.

2. Ideally, the traits that you look for in a vampire are...
a) Unconditional love, gorgeous looks and putting your needs before his own.
b) Chivalry, respect and a strict moral code.
c) Italian charm, able to go out in the sunshine, sensitive.

3. Why aren't you afraid your vampire will try to drain your blood?
a) Because he's vegetarian.
b) You know he can drink a blood substitute.
c) He promises not to.

4. How old would you like your vampire to be?
a) Around 110 years old – young, in vampire terms.
b) Closer to 175 years old – a bit more experienced.
c) About 160 years old – in the middle.

5. What superpower would you like to possess?
a) The ability to shield your loved ones from attack.
b) Being able to hear other people's thoughts.
c) None – my personality is enough.

6. What's your ideal love life?
a) Pure – one soulmate for life, forsaking all others.
b) Courted by a gentleman who'll kill to protect me.
c) Being fought over by two gorgeous brothers.

7. What might stand in your way?
a) Problems with an ancient ruling vampire coven.
b) Difficulties with a vampire sheriff.
c) An unruly sibling.

Mostly Cs: Stefan Salvatore – the Vampire Diaries vampire.
Mostly Bs: Bill Compton – the True Blood vampire.
Mostly As: Edward Cullen – the Twilight vampire.

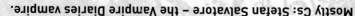

Your ideal vampire boyfriend is...

EDWARD CULLEN (THE *TWILIGHT* VAMPIRE)

You like your man to have a bit of sparkle. He'll be irrevocably drawn to your scent and without him you'll feel like your world will end. He might be a bit cold to the touch but you don't mind – you only care when his unconditional love for you causes you heartache as he breaks up with you for your own protection. Don't worry, though – he'll come back in the end. One day he might make all your dreams come true and let you join him in eternal life, but only when you're 100 per cent ready.

BILL COMPTON (THE *TRUE BLOOD* VAMPIRE)

You want a Southern gentleman, someone who'll always treat you well and respect your boundaries. Your natural charisma and naïveté makes it impossible for him to resist you but it also attracts the attention of other supernatural creatures, bringing out his protective instinct. He'll kill anyone who hurts you, and you know it.

STEFAN SALVATORE (*THE VAMPIRE DIARIES* VAMPIRE)

You prefer your boyfriend to have a sensitive side and to know the value of memories – after all, he's been writing his down in a journal for over 140 years. You have reawakened in this tortured soul the amazing feeling of being in love, and he resists drinking human blood even though it makes him weak. He wants nothing more than to live a normal human life and with you by his side, he feels as if he finally has that chance.

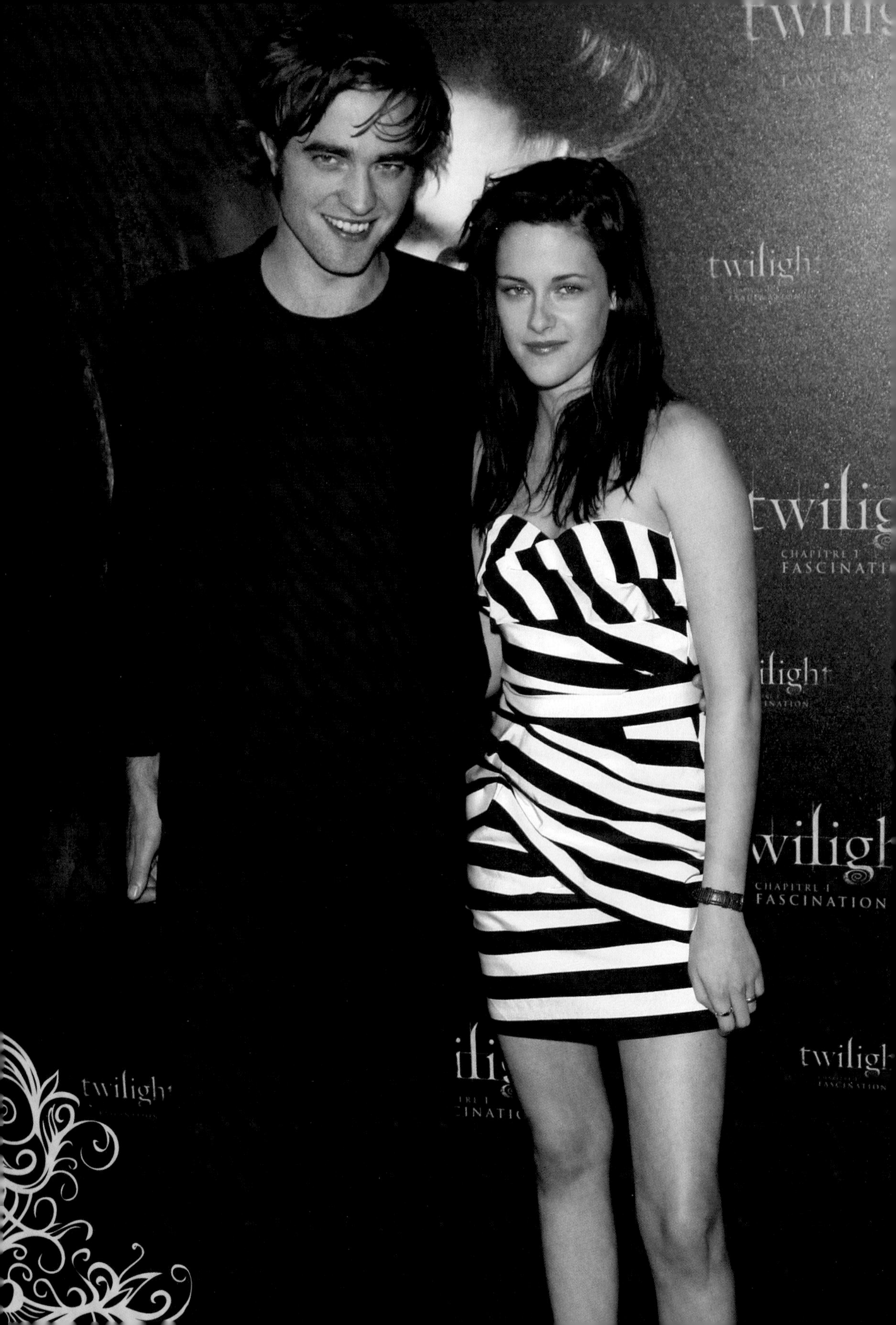
FASCINATION

TWILIGHT
THE TWILIGHT PHENOMENON

IT'S IMPOSSIBLE TO THINK ABOUT VAMPIRES WITHOUT THINKING OF *TWILIGHT*. THROUGH THE IMMENSE POPULARITY OF HER RIVETING *THE TWILIGHT SAGA* SERIES, AUTHOR STEPHENIE MEYER HAS CHANGED THE COURSE OF VAMPIRE MYTHOLOGY FOREVER.

She readily admits that her kind of vampire is different. 'In general, my vampires don't have fangs and they don't need them,' Stephenie revealed. 'You know, strong as they are, it's kind of unnecessary. They're fairly indestructible – wooden stakes and garlic are not going to get you anywhere. They don't sleep at all, they're never unconscious and the sunlight doesn't harm them – it just shows them for what they are because they sparkle in the sun.' She insisted on having these vampire traits preserved in the movie adaptation, meaning no fangs, no coffins and lots of sparkling.

In fact, in the *Twilight* books, the reason why there are so many myths about vampires and garlic, mirrors, crosses, etc. is because the vampires themselves spread the rumours to deflect attention, 'so that people would say, "Oh this person can't be a vampire because I can see them in the mirror, so I'm safe"' – a smart strategy to keep humans in the dark about the existence of vampires.

STEPHENIE'S VAMPS

The bloodsuckers in *Twilight* share a few unique characteristics, though. All vampires become incredibly beautiful once they are created and vampirism gives them superhuman speed, strength and agility. Vampires who drink human blood have red eyes, while 'vegetarians' like the Cullens have golden eyes. All vampire eyes turn black when they're hungry.

Carlisle Cullen speculated that if a human has a very strong natural ability in life then that ability is enhanced when they are turned into vampires. This is why he has such compassion as a vampire and is able to resist the temptation to drink human blood.

WANTED: PERMANENTLY CLOUDY SKIES

Twilight is set in the town of Forks, Washington, on the Olympic Peninsula. Stephenie Meyer chose it as the perfect setting for her first book because she 'needed someplace ridiculously rainy' since her vampires cannot appear in direct sunlight. The Olympic Peninsula happens to have the most rainfall in the US and so Forks was the perfect setting, even though Stephenie had never actually been there. When she finally did visit in the summer of 2004, it totally lived up to her expectations except for one thing: she was disappointed by how sunny it was while she was there!

WHAT'S IN A NAME?
STEPHENIE'S FIRST TITLE FOR HER BOOK WAS FORKS BUT CHANGED TO TWILIGHT ONCE SHE WAS SIGNED UP BY HER PUBLISHER: MEGAN TINGLEY AT LITTLE, BROWN.

SMASHING RECORDS

The first book, *Twilight*, came out on 5 October 2005. Since then, Stephenie has released three sequels – *New Moon*, *Eclipse* and *Breaking Dawn* – plus an *Eclipse* novella called *The Short Second Life of Bree Tanner*, published on 5 June 2010. Over 100 million copies of *The Twilight Saga* have sold worldwide and the books have been translated into 38 different languages. Altogether, the series has spent over 235 weeks on the *New York Times* Bestseller List. Phew, that's a lot of books!

TWILIGHT NICKNAMES
FANS OF THE SERIES ARE KNOWN AS 'TWIHARDS', 'TWILIGHTERS' OR 'TWIFANS' AND ARE OFTEN DIVIDED INTO TWO MAIN TEAMS: TEAM EDWARD OR TEAM JACOB. WHICH TEAM ARE YOU ON?

BLOCKBUSTER MOVIES

The film adaptations of the *Twilight* books have been just as successful. There's always a danger that the movie versions don't live up to the book fans' expectations, but a ton of thought went into making sure that didn't happen with *Twilight*. Along with Stephenie's long list of things they couldn't change, the producers – and director Catherine Hardwicke, in particular – worked hard to choose the right cast. We think they did a pretty good job! Both *New Moon* (directed by Chris Weitz) and *Eclipse* (directed by David Slade) received good critical and fan reviews.

BREAKING DAWN

The US release date for *Breaking Dawn: Part One* is 18 November 2011. There was a lot of buzz surrounding the choice of director and even more excitement when it was announced the book will be split into two movies. The director will be Bill Condon (*Dreamgirls*) and he wrote a letter to fans on Facebook to reassure everyone that he'll try his best to do the complicated final book justice. We'll just have to wait and see!

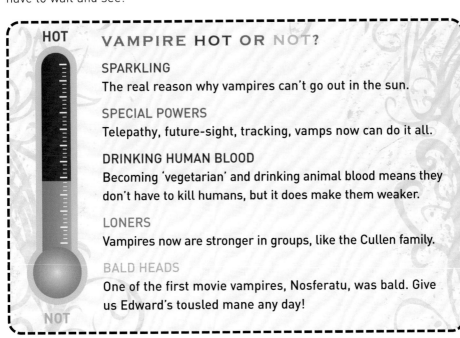

HOT

VAMPIRE HOT OR NOT?

SPARKLING
The real reason why vampires can't go out in the sun.

SPECIAL POWERS
Telepathy, future-sight, tracking, vamps now can do it all.

DRINKING HUMAN BLOOD
Becoming 'vegetarian' and drinking animal blood means they don't have to kill humans, but it does make them weaker.

LONERS
Vampires now are stronger in groups, like the Cullen family.

BALD HEADS
One of the first movie vampires, Nosferatu, was bald. Give us Edward's tousled mane any day!

NOT

'AS FOR WHY I SIGNED ON TO THIS MOVIE, I READ THE BOOK IN ONE DAY AND I WAS HOOKED... IT WAS VERY ROMEO AND JULIET. TWO LOVERS WHO FIND IT IMPOSSIBLE TO BE TOGETHER BECAUSE OF THE FAMILIES THEY COME FROM.'

– PETER FACINELLI (CARLISLE CULLEN) ON WHY HE LOVES *TWILIGHT*, EYEFORFILM.COM

BECOMING A TWILIGHT VAMPIRE

With Stephenie's rewriting of vampire lore, the stylists of the *Twilight* films had to stay away from more traditional bloodsucker looks. Principal make-up artist Jeanne Van Phue said, 'All of the vampires are pale, but I didn't want them to look ghoulish... I didn't want to contour, but I didn't want them to fade away, either.'

The constant rain provided an additional challenge – and Jeanne had to make sure the make-up was completely waterproof! 'Trying to fix make-up in the rain with a wet face and wet brush was difficult.'

VAMPIRE FILE – EDWARD CULLEN

FULL NAME: Edward Anthony Masen (he became Edward Cullen when he joined the Cullen family)
DATE OF BIRTH: 20 June 1901
AGE: 109
DATE OF VAMPIRE BIRTH: September 1918
ETERNAL AGE: 17
CREATOR: Carlisle Cullen
PLACE OF BIRTH: Chicago, Illinois
CURRENT RESIDENCE: Forks, Washington
HEIGHT: 6'2"
EYES: Once green, now golden/topaz
FAVOURITE FOOD: Mountain Lion
HOBBIES: Collecting cars, playing the piano
POWERS: Telepathy – he can read the minds of humans, vampires and shapeshifters – unless they have shielding abilities
WEAKNESSES: His love for Bella; gets weaker if he goes too long without drinking blood
ENEMIES: James, Victoria, the Volturi, certain members of the Quileute Wolf Pack
ETERNAL LOVE: Isabella Marie 'Bella' Swan
LOVE RIVAL: Jacob Black

NOTES ON EDWARD

Edward is the ultimate hero of *The Twilight Saga*. He's as close to perfection as a man can get – supernaturally beautiful, with bronze, unkempt hair and topaz eyes. Often Bella compares him to the Greek god Adonis and his skin is cold and hard to the touch, like marble.

Edward was saved from death by Carlisle Cullen. As a newborn, Edward can't control his need for human blood. Eventually, though, he joins Carlisle's vegetarian clan and vows to drink only from animals.

His vampire life lacks any purpose until Bella arrives. The scent of her blood is so tempting Edward almost breaks his century-old vow. Even once he has regained control of his hunger, he can't stay away from her, and the pair fall deeply in love.

Edward struggles with being a vampire and sees himself as a monster. He resists turning Bella into a vampire until the birth of their half-vampire/half-human daughter convinces him that it's the right decision.

HEARTTHROB – ROBERT PATTINSON

VITAL STATISTICS
FULL NAME: Robert Thomas Pattinson
BIRTHDAY: 13 May 1986
HOMETOWN: Barnes, London
PARENTS: Clare and Richard
SIBLINGS: Two older sisters, Lizzy and Victoria

Is there any actor with more amazing fans than Robert Pattinson? Rob was named one of *Time* magazine's 100 Most Influential People of the Year for 2010 and it's easy to see why – he's the most sought-after star in Hollywood right now.

LITTLE ROB

Rob only started going to acting classes because his dad thought it might help him meet some pretty girls! From a young age he knew that he would never fit in at a regular office job, but he thought he would pursue a career in music. He loves playing piano, which is one reason why Edward is shown playing piano in the movies – that's really Rob!

A MAGICAL MOMENT

Rob's acting career didn't get off to a great start – he was actually edited out of his first-ever movie, *Vanity Fair* – although you can catch his scenes, where he plays Reese Witherspoon's son, on the DVD extras! When he was 18, though, a magical role in the hugely successful *Harry Potter* franchise came his way as the doomed Hufflepuff heartthrob Cedric Diggory. 'Robert Pattinson was born to play the role,' commented *Goblet of Fire* director Mike Newell. 'He's quintessentially English, with chiselled public-schoolboy good looks.'

Rob could've been forgiven for thinking *Harry Potter* was to be the biggest franchise that he would ever star in – the next few movies he filmed were much smaller than *Harry Potter*. Luckily he had picked up some pointers on how to

handle superstardom from the three main actors from the franchise, especially Daniel Radcliffe. 'I guess [it helped] just seeing how the *Harry Potter* people have dealt with it, and they're still very, very normal and sane,' said Rob.

THE EDWARD FACTOR

After starring in several 'indie' films, Rob's agent convinced him to try out for a great part in a mainstream movie: Edward Cullen. But Rob found it really hard to see himself as Edward. Even though he thought the character could

> **'HOW DO YOU FIND THE BEST-LOOKING GUY IN THE WORLD THAT EVERYONE IS GOING TO THINK IS GREAT-LOOKING, BUT HE HAS TO BE BELIEVABLE TO BE A 17-YEAR-OLD IN HIGH SCHOOL?'**
> – CATHERINE HARDWICKE ON THE DIFFICULTIES OF CASTING EDWARD

have a lot of depth, he was concerned that he would just be cast as a pretty boy. 'The Edward in the book is like an enigma of everything that's perfect about a man,' he explained. 'I just couldn't figure out a way to act perfect; I felt like an idiot going into the audition.'

It was his co-star Kristen Stewart who convinced Rob to take the role. He was so impressed by her acting that he knew this was a project he wanted to be involved with. Stephenie Meyer loved him, calling him 'amazing', but at first fans of the book weren't happy with Rob being cast as Edward. There was a lot of backlash – until the movie came out and then the fans came to see him as the perfect Edward he is!

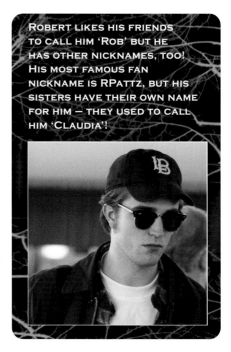

ROBERT LIKES HIS FRIENDS TO CALL HIM 'ROB' BUT HE HAS OTHER NICKNAMES, TOO! HIS MOST FAMOUS FAN NICKNAME IS RPATTZ, BUT HIS SISTERS HAVE THEIR OWN NAME FOR HIM — THEY USED TO CALL HIM 'CLAUDIA'!

BEING EDWARD

Actually 'becoming' Edward was a challenge for Rob as well. He had to wear coloured contacts every day and even had to wear a wig at first. Luckily, though, 'after studying his face and jaw line in the make-up test, the decision was made to go with short hair to accentuate his amazing jaw line,' revealed make-up artist Jeanne Van Phue. Fans everywhere breathed a deep sigh of relief!

TO THE FUTURE

Rob is so in demand at the moment. He's signed up to star in the movie adaptation of Guy de Maupassant's *Bel Ami* in 2011 as Georges Duroy, a 'totally amoral' young man who rises to power through seduction and cunning. The film is set in Paris in 1890, which means he gets to appear in old-fashioned costumes looking very dapper! He also has *Breaking Dawn* to appear in, so we're far from seeing the last of him yet.

VAMPIRE FILE – EMMETT CULLEN

FULL NAME: Emmett Dale McCarty
DATE OF BIRTH: 1915
AGE: 95
DATE OF VAMPIRE BIRTH: 1935
ETERNAL AGE: 20
CREATOR: Carlisle Cullen
PLACE OF BIRTH: Uncertain, but Rosalie found him in the Tennessee mountains
CURRENT RESIDENCE: Forks, Washington
HEIGHT: 6'5"
EYES: Golden
POWERS: Stronger than most vampires, enhanced speed and agility
WEAKNESSES: Likes to pick fights; gets weaker if he goes too long without drinking blood
ETERNAL LOVE: Rosalie Hale

NOTES ON EMMETT

Carlisle turned Emmett into a vampire. He was attacked by a bear in the Tennessee Mountains and found half-dead by Rosalie. She had to bring him to Carlisle because she didn't trust herself to turn him into a vampire without killing him. Emmett is now Rosalie's mate, the biggest and burliest of the Cullen clan. He loves to fight and relishes the battle against the newborns in *Eclipse*.

Kellan Lutz, who plays Emmett in the movies, just loves his character. 'Emmett's awesome,' said Kellan. 'He's the coolest character I think I could play as far as *Twilight* [is concerned]. He's just the fun-loving vampire. He just has fun cracking jokes at Bella and being the big brother to all the other family members.'

HEARTTHROB – KELLAN LUTZ

VITAL STATISTICS
FULL NAME: Kellan Christopher Lutz
DATE OF BIRTH: 15 March 1985
HOMETOWN: Dickinson, North Dakota
SIBLINGS: Three older brothers, three younger
brothers and one baby sister, Brittany

Kellan is no stranger to hard work. Growing up, he spent the holidays on his grandparents' farm in Iowa, where he helped to tear down and rebuild barns or drive the tractor. 'I'd rather do manual labour than sit behind a desk,' the adventurous Kellan told *Interview* magazine. Proving he has brains too, Kellan thought he would study chemical engineering at university or maybe become a Navy SEAL. Instead, he moved to LA, where his all-American good looks and fun personality helped get him a job at Abercrombie & Fitch – at first, selling clothes and then later modelling for the A&F catalogue.

FROM SOLDIER TO VAMPIRE

At acting classes in LA, Kellan found his passion. He began to appear in everything from TV dramas to music videos (did you see him in Hilary Duff's video for 'With Love'?). While playing a soldier in the miniseries *Generation Kill*, he heard about the *Twilight* movie and sent his audition tape out to Catherine Hardwicke. Later, she was to call him 'my perfect Emmett', which made him really happy.

Coming from such a large family has helped Kellan make Emmett Cullen the awesome character that he is – 'I feel like I am a lot like Emmett, and used my experiences from growing up in the Midwest and having such a big family, and I use that as I tap into Emmett.' He's super competitive with his brothers and once played a two-hour game of Wii sport tennis against one of them!

Because Emmett is supposed to be the biggest and buffest vampire on set, Kellan has to work out all the time. Luckily he enjoys doing push-ups! He also eats a lot of protein and is rumoured to have 16 eggs for breakfast.

> OFTEN KNOWN TO HIS FAMILY AS 'KRAZY KELLAN', KELLAN ALSO SAID THAT HE WOULD 'FEEL MOST FAMOUS WHEN PEOPLE ARE ABLE TO PRONOUNCE MY NAME RIGHT INSTEAD OF KAI-LAN OR KI-LON.' (HIS NAME RHYMES WITH HELEN, BY THE WAY!)

Next up he's set to play a god – Poseidon, to be exact, in *Immortals* on 11 November 2011. He's going to be joined by Henry Cavill (who was Stephenie Meyer's first choice for the role of Edward Cullen – Henry couldn't play Edward, though, because he was already too old!). Kellan's certainly god-like to us!

VAMPIRE FILE – CARLISLE CULLEN

FULL NAME: Carlisle Cullen
NICKNAME: Stregoni Benefici (meaning the vampire who is an ally to humans, mortal enemy of 'evil' vampires)
DATE OF BIRTH: 1640
AGE: 370
DATE OF VAMPIRE BIRTH: 1663
ETERNAL AGE: 23
CREATOR: An unnamed vampire whom Carlisle was trying to kill in his human life
PLACE OF BIRTH: London, England
CURRENT RESIDENCE: Forks, Washington
HEIGHT: 6'2"
OCCUPATION: Doctor
POWERS: Compassion; easily resists human blood
WEAKNESSES: His family
ETERNAL LOVE: His wife, Esme

NOTES ON CARLISLE

Carlisle Cullen was born in 1640 in London, England. His father hunted and killed supernatural creatures such as werewolves, witches and vampires. Carlisle didn't like to follow in his father's footsteps as he knew that he sometimes killed innocent people, but Carlisle tracked vampires all the same. In 1663, he was turned by one of the vampires he was trying to kill.

Since becoming a vampire, Carlisle has held a compassionate view of humans and is not interested in killing them or drinking their blood. The Volturi tried in vain to convert him to drinking human blood. He spent hundreds of years studying medicine and art, eventually moving to America, where he began to save select individuals from certain death – including his wife Esme and adopted son Edward.

Due to the massive collection of art and antiques that he has amassed throughout the centuries, he was recently voted the world's richest fictional character in *Forbes* Magazine. He is estimated to be worth $34.1 billion, having earned [a] doctor's salary for 340 years without paying for groceries, [or] health care expenses. [He] avoids sunshine and public displays of wealth, but owns several valuable properties, including [a] yacht, private island [and a] collection

HEARTTHROB – PETER FACINELLI

VITAL STATISTICS
DATE OF BIRTH: 26 November 1973
PARENTS: Bruna and Pierino Facinelli
HOMETOWN: Queens, New York
NATIONALITY: Italian-American
FAMILY: Jenny Garth (wife) and three daughters:
Luca Bella, Lola Ray and Fiona Eve

When Peter was a kid, he was worried that his
shyness would stop him from becoming an actor. 'One part of my brain said, "You
should go be an actor" and the other part of my brain said, "You're really nuts
because I can't even stand in the lunch line in school because I'm afraid of people."'

Luckily, Peter got over his shyness and has become really successful. He has
had small parts in lots of movies and shows, and his biggest role pre-*Twilight* was
as an undercover cop in the show *Fastlane* in 2002.

VAMPIRES, BLOOD AND GUTS

When Peter first heard about a vampire film from his agent, he wasn't interested:
'I was thinking blood and guts, something in the horror genre, so I said no.' It
wasn't until he realised it was a love story at heart that he wanted to audition.

PETER LOVES TWEETING AND HE
HAS OVER 1.6 MILLION
FOLLOWERS. 'I LOVE CONNECTING
WITH THE FANS,' HE SAYS.
'THEY'RE ALL SO DEDICATED AND
WONDERFUL TO ME THAT I LOVE
TO BE ABLE TO GIVE BACK.'
FOLLOW HIM @PETERFACINELLI

At first, they cast someone a lot older for Carlisle.
Peter was disappointed but grateful to have been
considered, so he sent director Catherine Hardwicke a
present: a book all about vampires in film. Eventually
when the other actor didn't work out, the gift reminded
Catherine of Peter and he was brought back for the role.
'I bought my way into *Twilight* for $29.90,' Peter jokes.

The biggest challenge he faced was portraying
Carlisle's 370 years. 'I did a lot of history research,' he explained. 'I wanted to learn
about the period he grew up in, and go through each decade where he might be
and where his travels took him. I felt that the way he moved and talked should
reflect someone from a different period, so those were the things that I worked on.'

He might only be a few years older than the rest of the cast, but Peter still acts
like a mentor to them. While most of the other actors are just starting out in their
careers, he has been building his for a long time. With *Twilight* giving him a whole
legion of new fans, Peter won't have any trouble in sustaining his career for as
long as he wants to!

VAMPIRE FILE – JASPER HALE

FULL NAME: Jasper Whitlock Hale
DATE OF BIRTH: 1843
AGE: 167
DATE OF VAMPIRE BIRTH: 1863
ETERNAL AGE: 20
CREATOR: Maria
PLACE OF BIRTH: Texas
Current Residence: Forks, Washington
HEIGHT: 6'3"
POWERS: He can manipulate emotions
WEAKNESSES: Finds it more difficult to be around humans, especially if they are bleeding
ETERNAL LOVE: Alice

America, which divided the northern and southern states. Jasper joined the Confederate Army as a teenager and quickly climbed up the ranks – so quickly in fact, that he attracted the attention of a vampire called Maria. She turned Jasper into a vampire to help her train an army of newborns. Maria also realises that he can manipulate emotions, making newborn vampires easier to deal with.

For a while, Jasper works with Maria until he tires of the constant bloodshed and war. He leaves and becomes a nomad, wandering around the US until he meets his future wife, Alice. She convinces him to move up to Forks and join the Cullen clan, forsaking human blood.

NE OF THE THINGS ABOUT JASPER IS HE DOESI
[HIS] ABILITY ALL THE TIME. IT'S SOMETHII
T HE'S VERY STRICT ABOUT USING BECAUSE I
E AN INVASION OF PRIVACY TO MAKE SOMEO
L SOMETHING, TO MANIPULATE EMOTIONS.'
– JACKSON RATHBONE ON JA

HEARTTHROB – JACKSON RATHBONE

VITAL STATISTICS
FULL NAME: Monroe Jackson Rathbone V
DATE OF BIRTH: 21 December 1984
HOMETOWN: Born in Singapore, but grew up in Midland, Texas
PARENTS: Randee Lynn and Monroe Jackson Rathbone IV
SIBLINGS: Three sisters – Ryann, Kelly and Britney

Jackson is a guy with tons of energy. 'The way I feel is that there's only 24 hours in a day, and I need at least 20 of them, so I sleep four hours a night,' he told Sci-Fi Wire. He definitely puts all those extra hours to good use, as Jackson is featured in two of the biggest films of 2010: *Eclipse* and *The Last Airbender*.

THE ACTING BUG

Jackson hit the ground running when he moved to LA and almost immediately got work with the Disney Channel interviewing other young Disney stars like Hilary Duff and Aly & AJ. He auditioned for the part of Edward but was eventually chosen to play Jasper. Jackson didn't mind as he felt a connection to the role because they were both from Texas: 'We both have a big Southern background and so that comes with the old-school qualities, such as taking a girl out or meeting people daily and talking to them,' he explained.

MUSICALLY INCLINED

Jackson balances his growing acting career with his other passion – music. He plays guitar (he named his guitar 'Annabelle'), piano, bass, mandolin and banjo, and has his own band – 100 Monkeys – whose sound is 'old-school rock and roll'. He even brought his guitar along to the audition for *Twilight*: 'I like to bring my guitar with me to auditions, it calms me down,' he says. His biggest role in between *Twilight*, called *The Last Airbender* from M. Night Shyamalan, has seen him gain even more recognition than before.

OTHER TWILIGHT HOTTIES

BLOODSUCKER – JAMES WITHERDALE

James was the main villain of the first *Twilight* movie and book. Once he had Bella's scent, he was determined to drink her blood. A supremely gifted tracker, he followed Bella back to Arizona, where he tried to kill her. Fortunately, Edward and the Cullens arrived just in time to stop him and James was killed by dismemberment and burning.

HEARTTHROB – CAM GIGANDET

Cam thought *Twilight* was such a good book that he considered making the movie himself before he found out about Catherine Hardwicke and Summit Entertainment. His girlfriend at the time persuaded him to read the books and he thought, 'We're going to make it ourselves. And then like two months later I found out that it was [already] being made. So it was pretty wild.' It's such a shame this gorgeous lad was killed off in the first movie, but don't worry: you can catch him opposite Christina Aguilera in *Burlesque* in November 2010.

BLOODSUCKER – RILEY BIERS

Riley is the first vampire created by Victoria in order to lead an army of newborn vampires back to Forks to kill Bella. He's in love with Victoria and will do anything for her. Xavier (see below) explained the mindset behind this complex character: 'He's harbouring extreme jealousy and hatred for humanity because that's exactly what he's been deprived of.'

HEARTTHROB – XAVIER SAMUEL

A new team is emerging…Team Newborn, and it's all down to this cutie from Australia! Xavier Samuel was born on 10 December 1983 and grew up in Adelaide, South Australia. *Eclipse* will be his first major Hollywood role and he beat out more established actors such as Chace Crawford and Tom Felton (who plays Draco Malfoy in *Harry Potter*) for the role. He's ready for superstardom and is looking to his co-stars for advice on how to react once the movie is released: 'They've done a good job keeping their wits in the whirlwind of it all, but also letting it get them where they want to be 'future-role' wise.'

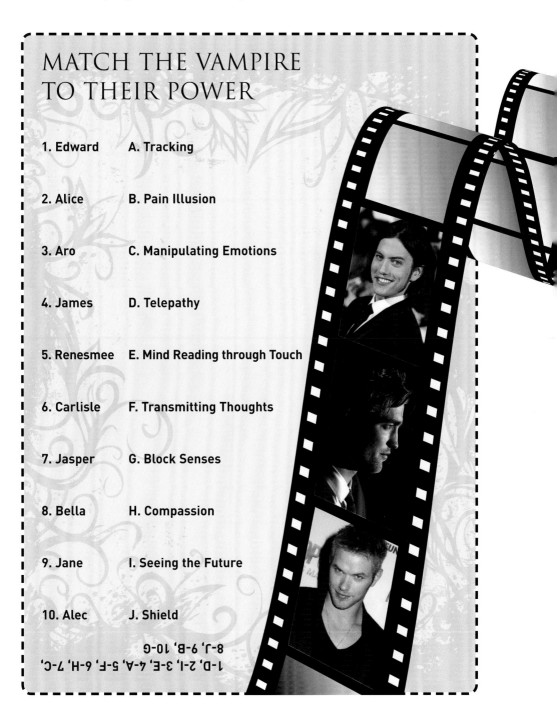

MATCH THE VAMPIRE TO THEIR POWER

1. Edward   A. Tracking

2. Alice   B. Pain Illusion

3. Aro   C. Manipulating Emotions

4. James   D. Telepathy

5. Renesmee   E. Mind Reading through Touch

6. Carlisle   F. Transmitting Thoughts

7. Jasper   G. Block Senses

8. Bella   H. Compassion

9. Jane   I. Seeing the Future

10. Alec   J. Shield

1-D, 2-I, 3-E, 4-A, 5-F, 6-H, 7-C, 8-J, 9-B, 10-G

TRUE BLOOD

WITH ITS SEXY, QUIRKY CAST, DARK TWISTS AND VERY ADULT SENSIBILITY, TRUE BLOOD STANDS OUT FROM THE CROWD OF VAMPIRE-RELATED TV SHOWS AND FILMS.

The programme is based on a series of best-selling books called *The Southern Vampire Mysteries* (or *The Sookie Stackhouse Novels*) by Charlaine Harris. Initially published in 2001, the books have enjoyed a massive resurgence in popularity since it began in 2008. The creator of the show is Alan Ball, who also devised HBO's popular show, *Six Feet Under*, so he's no stranger to finding success with gothic-themed television. He spotted the first book of the series, *Dead Until Dark*, in a bookstore before a dental appointment and was hooked. 'This wasn't a book I would normally read, but I couldn't put them down,' he said.

Charlaine was very open to having him adapt her books for a TV series and knew that he would stay close to her vision. Even so, it was inevitable there would be a few places where the show would differ from the books. 'The main story is the same. We diverge mostly in the secondary characters,' explained Alan. Overall, fans of the books have been extremely happy with how the show has complemented the book series.

> SO FAR THERE ARE TEN BOOKS IN *THE SOUTHERN VAMPIRE MYSTERIES* SERIES. THE LATEST, *DEAD IN THE FAMILY*, WAS RELEASED IN MAY 2010. BUT DON'T WORRY, *TRUE BLOOD* FANS: CHARLAINE IS CONTRACTED TO WRITE THREE MORE!

CHARLAINE'S VAMPS

True Blood vampires are much more traditional than the *Twilight* vampires. They have to sleep during daylight hours, they're hurt by silver, they have fangs... and they're not afraid to use them. They've been able to 'come out of the coffin' and reintegrate into society because a blood substitute (known as 'Tru Blood') has been developed in Japan, which they can drink to survive without draining humans. The vampires live in a very strict hierarchical society, where age and strength determines position and a younger vampire never defies his elders. These vampires can be killed if a wooden stake is plunged through their heart.

In a unique twist on the vampire myth, some humans desire vampire blood (nicknamed 'V') as much as the vampires are eager for human blood. V is an illegal drug that causes amazing hallucinations, can increase strength and heighten attractiveness. V-addicts hunt and drain vampires of their blood, restraining them

Author of *The Southern Vampire Mysteries*, Charlaine Harris.

with silver chains. As Stephen Moyer, who plays vampire Bill Compton, says, 'It isn't the vampire who is malevolent [in *True Blood*]; it's the human characters that have the flaws.'

CLEVER AD CAMPAIGNS

Alan Ball and the producers of *True Blood* launched the series in the viral marketing arena with gusto, coming up with tons of innovative ideas. They made a real version of the Tru Blood drink to sell online (it's a blood-orange soda) and put little cards in vending machines throughout the US, which read: 'Sold out of Tru Blood'. Some of the posters even came with wooden 'snap-off stakes' in the event of nearby vampires. They also took advantage of all sorts of viral marketing campaign tricks, making full use of Twitter, blogs and microsites to direct attention towards the show.

For the wait between seasons 2 and 3, the marketing people at True Blood used the ingenious slogan 'Waiting Sucks'. Every week or so they released a new poster or video teaser to keep eager fans intrigued about the upcoming season.

WHAT DOES YOUR BLOOD TYPE TASTE LIKE?
ACCORDING TO DIFFERENT FLAVOURS OF TRU BLOOD, TYPE A IS LIGHT AND DELICATE, TYPE B IS AGGRESSIVE AND ENERGISING, AB IS SMOOTH AND REFINED, WHILE TYPE O IS HEARTY AND SATISFYING. IT'S ALSO BEST SERVED WARM! ON THE TRUE BLOOD SET, THE 'BLOOD' THEY DRINK IS A SUGARCANE MIXTURE THAT TASTES LIKE 'STRAWBERRY-FLAVOURED CORN SYRUP', ACCORDING TO STEPHEN MOYER.

TV SUCCESS

True Blood is one of the most successful shows ever on the US network HBO, with 5.4 million people tuning in to watch the second season finale. It also sold more DVDs than any other TV show in 2009. Also, it's not just teens that love it: *True Blood* fans are spread across every age and generation! Stephen Moyer experiences the phenomenon firsthand: 'I go out in the street and I get spotted by septuagenarian [70-year-old] men, and they come up and tell me stories about the whole family coming to their house on a Sunday. Literally, three generations of men and their wives and their children and their extended family, and I think that's what the show has done.'

BECOMING A TRUE BLOOD VAMPIRE

The fangs designed for the *True Blood* vampires are located on the eyeteeth (right next to your front teeth). This puts them further forward, more like a snake than a wolf or bat. Each cast member has a set of plastic fangs, and they shoot scenes with, and without them – the transition is added in afterwards. Stephen thinks they are really uncomfortable to wear, similar to a retainer!

VAMPIRE FILE – BILL COMPTON

FULL NAME: William Thomas Compton
NICKNAME(S): Bill, Vampire Bill
DATE OF BIRTH: Sometime in 1835
AGE: 175
DATE OF VAMPIRE BIRTH: Just after the
American Civil War
VAMPIRE AGE: Early 30s
CREATOR: Lorena, a female vampire
PLACE OF BIRTH: Bon Temps, Louisiana
CURRENT RESIDENCE: Bon Temps, Louisiana
FAVE FLAVOUR OF BLOOD: O-neg Tru Blood,
a blood substitute
SUPERNATURAL POWERS: Glamouring, ability
to heal, super-strength and speed
BEST TRAITS: Chivalrous, a Southern gentleman; he has morals and ethics,
tries to 'mainstream' with humans and associate with them – not feed off them
WORST TRAITS: Possessive, willing to kill anyone who harms or threatens Sookie
ETERNAL LOVE: Sookie Stackhouse
VULNERABILITIES: Sunlight, silver, irritated by garlic
NOT BOTHERED BY: Crosses
LOVE RIVALS: Shapeshifter Sam, Eric (another vampire)
FANS' NICKNAMES: Bill's Babes, Moyer's Maidens

NOTES ON BILL

Bill Compton is the first vampire to 'come out of the coffin' in Bon Temps
Louisiana. The creation of the synthetic blood substitute Tru Blood gives him the
opportunity to 'mainstream' – to try and associate with humans and live a norma
life among them. He can think of no place better than to try and mainstream ir
his former home, where he once had a family.

With his striking blue eyes, pale skin and old-fashioned Southern charm, Bil
stands out from the crowd at Merlotte's bar. It's only feisty and telepathic waitress
Sookie Stackhouse who is curious (and brave) enough to approach him. Bil
courts Sookie in a very old-fashioned and proper way, and they fall in love. 'Apar
from the biting, their relationship is one of great love,' says Stephen

BILL IN THE BOOKS

In *The Southern Vampire Mysteries* series, Bill's birthday is 9 April 1840, making him a few years younger than Bill from *True Blood*, and on 20 November 1868, Lorena turns him into a vampire. The producers of the TV show were conscious they didn't want to make Bill exactly like the books, as this would mean that the show was too predictable. 'You want to surprise the fans, keep people guessing,' said Stephen.

In person, Stephen Moyer always takes people by surprise. While 'vampire Bill' is a dark-haired, pale-skinned vampire from the Deep South – complete with slow, seductive Southern drawl – in real life, Stephen is an Essex boy with a broad British accent. Even though he now spends most of his time in LA, he still considers his house near Hampstead Heath, north London, to be his home.

EARLY LIFE

Stephen's love for acting started young. His first acting role was the lead in a school production of Tom Sawyer – his headmaster offered him the part – and from there on, he didn't look back. 'I played the lead in most of the school plays, and I kind of knew, then and there, that I wanted [to act], from about the age of 13.'

As a teen, he loved the music of Paul Weller and dressed in the popular 'mod revival' fashion of the 1980s – a smooth, sophisticated look with sharp suits, button-down shirts and skinny ties.

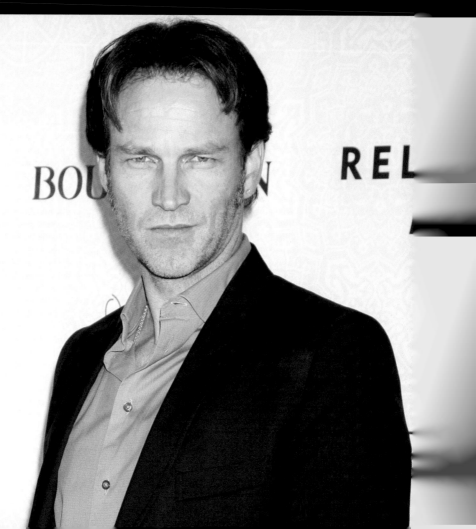

VITAL STATISTICS
FULL NAME: Stephen John Emery
DATE OF BIRTH: 11 October 1969
HOMETOWN: Herongate, near Brentwood, Essex
MARITAL STATUS: Engaged to actress Anna Paquin
KIDS: Billy and Lilac

While most of his classmates considered careers in the City as bankers or lawyers, Stephen wanted to continue acting. In his small hometown, that dream was almost unheard of and so he didn't have anyone that he could turn to for advice or whose footsteps he might follow in. Instead he picked up a magazine for actors and found an advertisement for a stage school at the back. He applied and after several auditions, landed a place at the London Academy of Music and Dramatic Art (LAMDA).

His childhood training in school plays and at the Brentwood Theatre Club had prepared him well and Stephen progressed smoothly into working as a professional actor. He spent several years playing Romeo in Shakespeare's Romeo and Juliet – experience that would come in handy later on down the line as another tragic love hero, Bill Compton.

Stephen's next challenge was to break into television and film. He became a fixture of British TV, acting on popular shows such as *Casualty*, *Midsomer Murders* and *Waking the Dead*. When he booked the title role in *Prince Valiant* (1997), working with *Grey's Anatomy's* Katherine Heigl, he must have thought his big movie break had surely come, but it wasn't to be. Even though he managed to consistently find work and was building up to bigger and bigger roles, he hadn't yet found the platform to launch himself into superstardom. Ultimately, he had to wait for the role with the right amount of bite.

WHAT'S IN A NAME? Before Stephen could start acting, he needed to join Equity, the British actor's union. But another 'Stephen Emery' had got there first. Not only that, the only acting his namesake had done at that time was playing the back end of a horse! At least casting directors wouldn't get confused after he chose the surname 'Moyer' and he hasn't looked back since.

A TASTE OF SOMETHING NEW

Stephen was almost ready to give up on Hollywood and his dream of breaking out as a big star on American TV. Also, he missed his children back home in England and wanted to spend more time with them. But just as he was about to throw it all in and concentrate on building a career in the UK, his agent persuaded him to read one more script, saying, 'I won't make you read any other scripts, but just read this one. Everybody is talking about it.'

That script was *True Blood* and the sexy tale of Southern vampires won him over. He immediately sent a video – complete with a Southern accent that he made up on the spot – to the producers over in America.

The producers, especially the show's creator Alan Ball, loved Stephen and asked him to fly out to LA the next day. For him it was a surreal moment as things at home had hit a dramatic low point: the very same day, his home had been burgled. 'My entire house had been ransacked,' he explained. 'Everything taken...

> **'IT WAS SEXY AND ROMANTIC... THERE WAS THIS KIND OF EDGE TO IT AS WELL. AND I KNEW RIGHT THEN THAT THIS COULD BE AMAZING.'**
> – STEPHEN, ON HIS FIRST READ OF THE *TRUE BLOOD* SCRIPT

My son and daughter ran into their bedrooms to see what had happened. Lilac said, "They haven't stolen our duvet!" And my son said, "They haven't stolen our teddy bears, Daddy!" And I was hugging them, and about an hour later, I got a phone call to say, "Alan wants to meet you. Can you fly tomorrow?" It was a very interesting few days.'

TRUE BLOOD...TRUE LOVE

When Stephen arrived in the US for the auditions, he also met Anna Paquin for the first time. He was at once taken by the (at the time) dark-haired beauty but couldn't imagine either of them landing the parts of Bill and Sookie. Stephen had just finished filming a show that required him to play a surfer dude, complete with bronzed skin and bleached hair. Anna, on the other hand, had raven-black hair and pale skin – the total opposite of blonde, tanned, Southern belle Sookie Stackhouse, as described in the novels and in the script.

But Alan Ball saw that Stephen and Anna had the one thing that would make the show a success: chemistry. Hair and tan colour could be changed, but what was most important was that the two leads were convincing as a couple defying the supernatural odds.

Almost immediately, the two started dating – their first date was at a hole-in-the-wall sushi restaurant in LA – but they kept their relationship under wraps for almost 10 months. 'Neither of us wanted our relationship to be the story,' explained Stephen. Only when they knew they were serious about each other and ready to get engaged did they come out as a couple – to the delight of fans everywhere.

OTHERWORLDLY MUSINGS

Transforming into a vampire each day seems to have had a mysterious effect on Stephen. Indeed, he's become more in tune with his supernatural side since working on *True Blood*: 'If you'd asked me if I believed in the paranormal this time last year I'd have said no. I used to be an atheist, but I've chilled out a bit on that. A couple of things in the past year have made me think maybe there is something to it.'

VAMPIRE FILE – ERIC NORTHMAN

FULL NAME: Eric Northman
NICKNAME(S): Eric the Northman, Leif
DATE OF BIRTH: 1046
AGE: 964
DATE OF VAMPIRE BIRTH: 1077
ETERNAL AGE: 31
CREATOR: Godric
PLACE OF BIRTH: Norway
CURRENT RESIDENCE: Shreveport, Louisiana
FAVE BLOOD FLAVOUR: Human
OCCUPATION: Owns vampire bar Fangtasia, Sheriff of Louisiana Area 5

NOTES ON ERIC

Eric is by far the oldest vampire in *True Blood*. Born in Scandinavia during the Viking era, he joined a rogue group of warriors and disappeared in the midst of battle in 1077. Mortally wounded, he was turned into a vampire by Godric. He is now the Sheriff of Louisiana Area 5, enforcing vampire law in that area, and answers to Sophie-Anne Leclerq, Queen of Louisiana. Eric is also the creator of Pam, who helps him run Fangtasia.

ERIC IN PRINT

Eric is even older in the *True Blood* books, at least 1,000 years old. He is turned by a Roman vampire named Appius and has a human wife (Aude) along with six children. He and Sookie also have a very interesting relationship throughout the books that might be drawn upon later in the TV series.

HEARTTHROB: ALEXANDER SKARSGÅRD

FULL NAME: Alexander (Alex) Johan Hjalmar Skarsgård
DATE OF BIRTH: 25 August 1976
HOMETOWN: Stockholm, Sweden
PARENTS: Stellan and My
SIBLINGS: He's the eldest of four brothers (Gustaf, Sam, Bill and Walter), one sister (Eija) and one half-brother (Ossian)

SWEDEN'S SEXIEST

Alex followed in the footsteps of his famous dad (who has appeared in *Pirates of the Caribbean* and *Mamma Mia!*) and started acting from a young age. On reaching his teens, however, he already felt burnt out of the acting world.

As a change of scene, he joined the military. 'Sweden is probably one of the three countries least likely to get in a war, so the military's pretty safe,' he explained. In fact, the 'missions' that he went on were so dull that the experience caused him to reconsider acting as a career: 'It gave me a lot of time to think about things. I realised I missed being onstage and on a set.'

> **ALEX HAS BEEN VOTED SEXIEST MAN ALIVE IN SWEDEN FIVE TIMES – AND WHO CAN BLAME THEM?**

ERIC THE VIKING

While slowly building up a steady fan base in Sweden and appearing in many Swedish films and plays, Alex would jet over to Los Angeles to audition for bigger parts. He scored his first major role on American TV, playing Sergeant Brad Colbert in the miniseries *Generation Kill* alongside another vampire – Kellan Lutz. It was while basking in the heat of Mozambique that Alex sent off his audition tape for *True Blood*, initially for the part of Bill.

> **FAMILY CONNECTION**
> ALEX AND HIS DAD STELLAN APPEAR IN A FEW MOVIES TOGETHER. BOTH HAVE JOINED THE VOICE CAST OF 3D ANIMATED FILM *MOOMINS* AND *THE COMET CHASE* AND CREEPY SCI-FI FLICK *METROPIA*.

Though Alex wasn't right for Bill, he made such an impression on creator Alan Ball that he brought him on to play the deadly Eric. In a recent interview with MTV, when asked how long he would want the series to run for, Alex's answer showed just how passionate he is about the show: 'I don't know – 45 years?! I'm having a blast, so hopefully we'll get to do it for a while. I love this show and my character.'

THE VAMPIRE DIARIES

THE *VAMPIRE DIARIES* IS THE NEWEST SHOW ON THE SUPERNATURAL-FANTASY HORROR BLOCK, ALTHOUGH IT'S BASED ON THE OLDEST SET OF BOOKS (THE FIRST WAS PUBLISHED IN 1991 AND THE SERIES WAS WRITTEN BY LISA JANE SMITH). IN SEPTEMBER 2009 THE SHOW PREMIÈRED TO RECORD RATINGS FOR US TV NETWORK, THE CW.

The brains behind the show, Kevin Williamson, knows teens: he created nineties mega-hits such as *Dawson's Creek* and the *Scream* movies. Williamson realised that a carbon copy of *Twilight* just wouldn't go down well with audiences, but that's why he liked *The Vampire Diaries* – he and co-creator Julie Pec saw so much potential there. The books were also less about one central relationship, like Bella and Edward, and more about a whole community. 'We're really sort of telling the story about a small town, all the darkness that lies underneath this town and how this vampire comes to town and sort of stirs it all up,' explained Kevin.

And he wasn't afraid to switch things up from the books – something that the fans initially weren't happy about. *The Vampire Diaries* differs a lot more from the original source material than *True Blood* or *Twilight*. One big change was making the lead girl a brunette, but Kevin explained this decision-making: 'Elena is an unlikable, selfish mean girl [in the books], but we had to make her accessible; you can't have that kind of character [lead] on a show – you have to like her. And that's why everyone's upset that we didn't cast a blonde.'

NOT ANOTHER TWILIGHT!

At first look, *The Vampire Diaries* does seem really similar to *Twilight*: a young girl falls in love with a hot, mysterious guy on the first day of school only to discover that he has a dark secret – the initial plot does seem to overlap. But Kevin Williamson likes to poke fun at this comparison by referencing the similarity in the episodes. 'These are kids who live in the real world,' he said, 'and so they read the books, they've seen the [*Twilight*] movies. You know, when one character finally finds out he's a vampire, the first question is, "Why don't you sparkle? Why don't you sparkle, I don't get it?" We even have a moment where Ian is reading, he's flipping through a book and he goes, "I just don't understand this Bella chick." So we have fun with it.'

Some vampire problems are universal – as long as Elena is human, Stefan will remain 17 while she grows older. But Kevin has seven books of material to draw from and at least three seasons already planned out, so he's confident he can keep it fresh.

BECOMING A VAMPIRE DIARIES VAMPIRE

The vampires in *The Vampire Diaries* have it a lot easier than some! With their special rings made of lapis lazuli, Stefan and Damon Salvatore are able to walk about in the sunshine. As far as the actors themselves are concerned, it means they're free to go to the beach and top up their tans whenever they want to. 'Our vampires don't really have any pale qualities other than when they turn and their teeth come out and their eyes turn red,' explained Paul Wesley (Stefan). 'So, I never really have to worry about [tanning]. I can go out in the sun. Continuity-wise, I have to worry about that, but I don't have to be pale.'

Although *The Vampire Diaries* vamps walk around in the sun, don't be fooled into thinking they're wimps – they become total monsters in the presence of blood. 'They're angry,' said writer Kevin Williamson. 'Any sort of hot emotion, anger, love, sex, anything that's really heightened and the blood rushes to the eyes. You see the blood rush into the eyes and then the teeth come out.' He wanted to make sure his characters looked terrifying so that there was a real contrast between Stefan's controlled, restrained vampire nature and Damon's (Ian Somerhalder) more animalistic and unpredictable tendencies.

Paul explained what it takes to become a truly scary monster: 'There's a lot of CGI [Computer-Generated Imagery], and some make-up around the eyes. I put some crazy contact lenses in. They put these four dots on my face, for the CGI guys to use as markers in post-production. I think that's how they do it in *True Blood* as well. It's actually very funny, because we do these scenes and Nina has to pretend to be in love with me, and I'm standing there with polka-dots on my face.'

VAMPIRE FILE – STEFAN SALVATORE

FULL NAME: Stefan Salvatore
DATE OF BIRTH: 1847
AGE: 163
DATE OF VAMPIRE BIRTH: Sometime in 1864
ETERNAL AGE: 17
CREATOR: Katherine Pierce
PLACE OF BIRTH: Mystic Falls, Virginia
CURRENT RESIDENCE: Mystic Falls, Virginia
STYLE: Rose tattoo on his right shoulder
BLOOD SUBSTITUTE: Animals
SUPERNATURAL POWERS: Superhuman strength and agility, enhanced hearing, influence on people's minds
BEST TRAITS: Refuses to drink human blood or use his powers on them, devotion to Elena
WORST TRAITS: Blood-red eyes and pale, veiny skin when he becomes a vampire
ETERNAL LOVE: Elena Gilbert
VULNERABILITIES: Drinking animal blood makes him weaker than other vampires, anti-vampire herb vervain, wooden bullets or stakes, sunlight (without his ring)
ENEMIES: His brother Damon.
LOVE RIVALS: Damon.

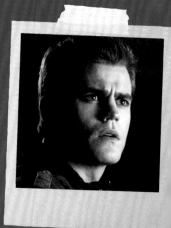

NOTES ON STEFAN

Stefan is the younger of the two Salvatore brothers and more sensitive brooding – it is Stefan who keeps a diary of his life throughout the ages. He is and raised in Mystic Falls, Virginia, and is turned just before the end American Civil War by female vampire Katherine Pierce. Katherine also t his brother Damon – she couldn't choose between the two of them.

Stefan shuns the typical vampire life and refuses to feed off humans though this makes his powers substantially weaker. Every couple of yea returns to Mystic Falls to check on his hometown. It's during one of homecomings that he sees Elena and is convinced to try to start life ane

STEFAN IN PRINT

In the books, Stefan is much older – over 500 years, in fact. Born in 1474 in Florence, Italy, he falls in love with a beautiful woman named Katherine von Schwartzschild, who happens to be a vampire. As a token of love, he drinks some of her blood. When he is 'killed' by his older brother Damon, he has too much of Katherine's blood inside him and he is subsequently turned into a vampire. As in the TV series, he doesn't like to drink human blood.

Five hundred years later, he moves to Fell's Church, Virginia, where he meets Elena – who is identical in looks to Katherine – and discovers his true soulmate.

Paul Wesley is no stranger to playing paranormal characters. Aside from brooding vampire Stefan Salvatore, he's also played a werewolf and a nephilim – a half-human, half-angel. It must have something to do with those classic good looks and killer stare.

At 29, he's older than your average high-schooler; yet considering Stefan is supposed to be 165 years old, Paul plays him with the kind of maturity that can only come with experience. His more refined style sets him apart from the juvenile antics of other high-school boys.

TRANSIENT LIFESTYLE

Paul didn't enjoy a normal high-school life – he changed schools three times and never found a solid group of friends. 'I was a bit of a troublemaker,' he explained. 'The first school I went to was an all-boys private Christian school

and it was all jocks and I don't think the teachers liked me.' He didn't like the rigidity of having to wear a uniform every day and so he switched to a public high school.

At 15, he landed a role in the long-running soap, *Guiding Light*. The series involved him travelling back and forth to New York for filming, so he could only come to class once a week. His poor attendance didn't go down well in school and appearing on TV isolated him from his fellow students. He transferred to Lakewood Prep, a place where they were happy for him to juggle acting and still graduate with a high-school diploma. Luckily he kept the same girlfriend all through high-school years so she helped maintain some stability in his life. Something else good came from moving around so much: the experience allowed him to better identify with his character Stefan, who is the 'new guy' at Mystic Falls High.

VITAL STATISTICS
FULL NAME: Paul Thomas Wasilewski
DATE OF BIRTH: 23 July 1982
HOMETOWN: New Brunswick, New Jersey
NATIONALITY: Polish and American
PARENTS: Agnieszka and Tomasz Wasilewski
SIBLINGS: Older sister Monika and two younger
sisters, Julia and Leah

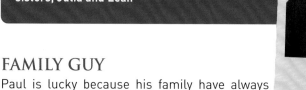

FAMILY GUY

Paul is lucky because his family have always supported him through everything. 'I'm the No. 1 supporter of following your passion,' declares Agnieszka, his mother. 'I believe that if you have something that you really want to do, I'm not going to tell you that you have to stay in school first. He can always go back to school. I want to be proud of him, which I already am, but my only wish is for him to be happy.' Younger sisters Julia and Leah are his biggest fans – they love *The Vampire Diaries*, too!

OUT-OF-THIS-WORLD ROLES

One of Paul's first major parts was as Luke Cates in the short-running series, *Wolf Lake*. He had a lot of fun playing a werewolf as it's wildly different to the restrained, intellectual vampire: 'When I was playing the werewolf, I was like 18 years old, and I think I was just like this teen who was running rampant. And I had a great time, and it fits the character perfectly, this alpha male machismo... that was me.'

WHAT'S IN A NAME? PAUL'S POLISH LAST NAME — WASILEWSKI — WAS JUST TOO HARD FOR PEOPLE TO PRONOUNCE AND SO HE ALTERED IT TO WESLEY. 'I ASKED MY FAMILY'S PERMISSION TO CHANGE IT, AND IT'S REALLY HELPED MY CAREER,' HE EXPLAINED TO *SOAP OPERA DIGEST*.

Divine intervention helped secure a different paranormal role, this time as an angel. Like *The Vampire Diaries*, *Fallen* is based on a popular series of books. Paul was cast as Aaron Corbett, who discovers on his eighteenth birthday that he can speak to animals as well as in any human language. 'He finds out that he's actually a nephilim, which is a half-human, half-angel,' explained Paul. 'Then he finds out that there are these powers that are sent to kill him and any other nephilim. It's an interesting mythological/action/adventure show and I'm really proud of it.'

Some of the most fun that he has ever had on set was in playing supernatural creatures so when news of a casting call for a hot, new vampire show came his way, he knew he wouldn't be able to resist.

DIARY OF A VAMPIRE

Paul has never worked so hard for a role in any show as for *The Vampire Diaries*. When he initially read the script, he thought that Damon was the part for him: 'I auditioned for the role of Damon three times, four times maybe. Constantly went back for Damon, back and forth, back and forth. They wouldn't see me for Stefan – they thought I wasn't right for it.

'EVERYONE WAS GREAT, BUT PAUL HAD THIS OLD SOUL, LIKE A HISTORY THAT YOU COULD FEEL. HE SEEMED LIKE HE'D BEEN AROUND LONGER, AND KNEW MORE, AND HE HAD A GRASP FOR THE CHARACTER DIFFERENT FROM ANYONE ELSE.'

– NINA DOBREV (ELENA) ON PAUL'S INCREDIBLE AUDITION FOR STEFAN SALVATORE

Then they went older for Damon, they passed it to Ian, and they go, "Maybe this will work." They brought me in for Stefan and I read for it like, four times.'

Actors from all over the world sensed the part could be big. As a result, Wesley faced some tough competition. 'I had to screen test against like, three guys from Australia, three guys from London, four guys from New York, five guys from LA. It was like *American Idol*. It was like, "Go home, go home..." and "You stay, you stay..."'

There was an initial backlash to the casting of Paul as Stefan Salvatore; as with Robert Pattinson, however, fans soon began to see why he was so right for the part. Paul's unconventional upbringing had a lot to do with making him an 'old soul' – he knew what it was like to be rejected, from schools and from shows, and he understood that the only way he would succeed was through hard work and by taking advantage of every opportunity.

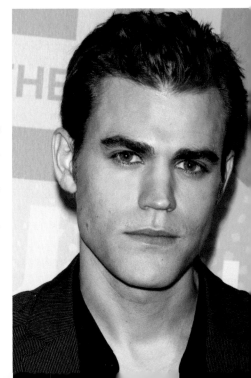

THE VAMPIRE DIARIES... AND BEYOND

The Vampire Diaries has finally given Paul the recognition he deserves after years of trying to score a starring role, but still allows him to have some independence. He's focused on the show at the moment, but took the time out to film a wildlife movie called *Beneath the Blue*. In his free time, he loves to travel and explore, especially in Atlanta, Georgia, where he now lives.

But Paul doesn't mind all the attention from fans, even if it means it's more difficult for him to explore anonymously. 'It's flattering,' he said, about the havoc caused by fans. 'I love what I do, and if people are responding to it, and if they do indeed respond to my character in such a positive way, I'm doing something right. So, for me, it just feels good.'

FIVE THINGS YOU MIGHT NOT KNOW ABOUT PAUL WESLEY

- DESPITE BEING IN TONS OF SHOWS, HE'S NEVER REALLY OWNED A TV.
- HE HAS NATURALLY POINTY TEETH. 'YOU'D THINK IT WOULD HAVE [HELPED GET ME THE ROLE] BUT THEY DIDN'T NOTICE IT UNTIL I WAS ON SET. THEN THEY WERE LIKE, "OH MY GOD, WHAT ARE THE ODDS?!"'
- HIS FAVOURITE BOOK IS J.D. SALINGER'S THE CATCHER IN THE RYE AND HIS DREAM ROLE WOULD BE THE NOVEL'S PROTAGONIST, HOLDEN CAULFIELD.
- HE LOVES WINTER SPORTS, ESPECIALLY ICE HOCKEY. 'I PLAYED ICE HOCKEY OBSESSIVELY FOR 14 YEARS OF MY LIFE,' HE SAYS.
- PAUL'S ALSO REALLY INTO POKER: 'I THINK [POKER] APPEALS TO ACTORS BECAUSE IT'S A PSYCHOLOGICAL GAME AND WHAT WE DO IS VERY PSYCHOLOGICAL. I MEAN, ESSENTIALLY, IF YOU HAVE A GREAT HAND, YOU DO EVERYTHING YOU CAN TO ACT LIKE YOU DON'T HAVE A GREAT HAND. IF YOU DON'T HAVE A GREAT HAND, YOU HAVE TO PRETEND. YOU REALLY HAVE TO FEEL OUT YOUR OPPONENT AND YOU REALLY HAVE TO SORT OF GET INTO THE MIND-SET. IT'S ACTUALLY KIND OF A SPIRITUAL THING. YOU REALLY HAVE TO BE TAPPED INTO YOUR SENSES; YOU'VE GOT TO BE ON TOP OF YOUR GAME.'

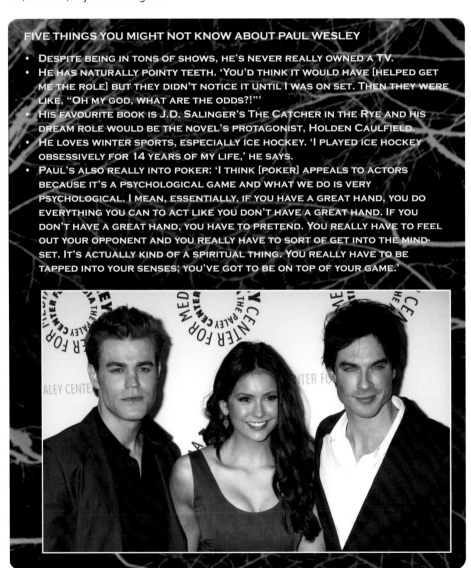

VAMPIRE FILE – DAMON SALVATORE

FULL NAME: Damon Salvatore
DATE OF BIRTH: Unknown
AGE: Over 170
DATE OF VAMPIRE BIRTH: Sometime in 1864
ETERNAL AGE: Approximately 25
CREATOR: Katherine Pierce
PLACE OF BIRTH: Mystic Falls, Virginia
CURRENT RESIDENCE: Mystic Falls, Virginia
FAVOURITE FLAVOUR OF BLOOD: Human
SUPERNATURAL POWERS: Superhuman strength and agility, enhanced hearing, influence on people's minds, can control fog and certain animals such as crows
BEST TRAITS: Not many! He is very powerful because he feeds on humans
WORST TRAITS: Ruthless, arrogant, enjoys killing
ETERNAL LOVE: Katherine, although he battles for Elena's affections, too
VULNERABILITIES: Anti-vampire herb vervain, wooden bullets or stakes, sunlight (without his ring)
ENEMIES: His brother Stefan
LOVE RIVALS: Stefan

NOTES ON DAMON

Damon is the opposite of his brother Stefan: he embraces afterlife as a vampire and treats humans with disdain. He kills at random when he needs to feed and doesn't care about causing mass amounts of chaos in a small community.

Damon returns to Mystic Falls to find out what his brother is up to, and is equally intrigued by Elena, who seems to be a reincarnation of his former lover and creator, Katherine. He decides to remain in Mystic Falls to generally wreak havoc in his brother's life but also to find out more about his long-lost love, Katherine. Could this bad boy have a good side? Actor Ian Somerhalder thinks so, saying: 'There are moments where you may see some sort of humanity in him, and there are moments when you may see that he may not be as intense as he appears to be.'

DAMON IN PRINT

In the books, Damon is born in fifteenth-century Florence, Italy. He is very evil and hates his brother. The most current *Vampire Diaries* book, *The Return*, features him as the central protagonist.

With his piercing blue eyes and sculpted features, it's not surprising that Ian Somerhalder's first job was as a model. He started modelling at the age of 10 and worked for Gucci, Versace and Calvin Klein, but he doesn't like being typecast as just another pretty face and takes his acting career very seriously, having studied the craft in New York for a long time.

VAMPIRE NATION

Although he grew up in Covington, Louisiana, Ian considers himself a New Orleans boy. New Orleans is famous for its rich gothic heritage and has its own, very special vampire connection: Anne Rice. Anne is the author of the novel, *Interview with the Vampire*, which introduced one of the world's most famous vampires: Lestat. Naturally, Ian couldn't grow up in New Orleans without being influenced by the vampire phenomenon. 'There's this mystique in New Orleans,' he explained. 'there's a mystical, vampirical thing about it. It was always there, and it's very underlying there. There's something about it that's really interesting, enticing, dangerous and sexy.'

LOST BOY

Ian Somerhalder's first big break came with the massive TV drama series *Lost*. As Boone Carlyle, he was one of the first survivors to be cast – and he was also the first to be killed off. He did get to come back at the start of Season 6, however, and his memorable performance kept him alive in the audience's imagination.

After his swift exit from the show, Ian too began to feel... well, a bit lost! He wasn't sure where to go next. Finally a role grabbed his attention, but it wasn't for *The Vampire Diaries*, it was in *True Blood*. He auditioned for the role of Sookie Stackhouse's brother Jason, but he didn't get it and was gutted. In the end this freed him up for an even juicier role... and everyone knows it's the bloodsuckers, not the humans, who get the most attention.

THE BAD BOY

After being turned down for *True Blood*, Ian didn't want any more to do with vampires. He was even sceptical about *The Vampire Diaries*, but after reading the part of Damon, he knew immediately that it was for him. 'I desperately wanted it,' he recalls, but he thought that he had missed the audition deadline. Luckily he hadn't, but he had to drive all the way from Las Vegas to LA – a 300-mile trip – in the early morning in order to make it on time, memorising the script along the way.

He might have had a bit more time to relax and get into the role, had Kevin Williamson been more direct with him right from the start. Kevin said, 'You know what, with Damon, as soon as I heard Ian Somerhalder was interested in the part, as far as I was concerned, he had it.' But Ian was so desperate for the role that he almost blew it at the final hurdle. 'Everyone said oh, he's definitely got the look, he looks like Damon, but he just didn't bring it when he read,' explained Kevin. 'Still, I knew he had it in him... Ian was a gamble. We took a gamble on him, and he delivered.'

BROTHERS GRIM

Ian Somerhalder and Paul Wesley may have to pretend to hate each other in character, but in real life they get along really well. 'We love each other, we are like brothers,' Ian told *iF* magazine. 'Paul is such a phenomenally talented, committed actor, and he's my good friend, and we could be doing this with anybody else and we got lucky. We worked really hard to get these roles and we're going to continue to work even harder to keep them.'

FAN LOVE

Ian is used to being on shows with a massive following – *Lost* is one of the biggest series of the twenty-first century – but he sees *The Vampire Diaries* on a different scale as it has all been driven by youth culture. Ian loves that teens are so active and vocal about their love for the show, including voting *The Vampire Diaries* as the winner of the People's Choice award. Ian's a great fan of Twitter: 'We know that this is such a great way to talk with fans, it's insane. You can push a button and a hundred thousand people will get that instantly.'

YOU CAN FOLLOW THE VAMPIRE DIARIES CAST ON TWITTER! IAN IS @IANSOMERHALDER AND NINA DOBREV IS @NINADOBREV.

Of course we know it's not all Robert, Stephen and Damon: Every generation has its popular vampire. Here's just a few...

NOSFERATU (1922) AND DRACULA (1931)

Nosferatu, eine Symphonie des Grauens was a German film and introduced one of the first vampires ever to appear on the big screen. This unauthorised adaptation of Bram Stoker's *Dracula* novel featured Max Schrek as Count Graf Orlok. A few years later, an official movie was made of the *Dracula* story, featuring Bela Lugosi in the title role.

HAMMER HORROR (1950s)

During the fifties, a production company called Hammer Films capitalised on the public's increasing love of horror movies and worked on a retelling of the Dracula story. Christopher Lee played an iconic Dracula in the initial film and its various sequels.

THE LOST BOYS (1987)

This eighties flick is seen as the main forerunner to teen vampire movies such as *Twilight*. The tagline was specifically written to appeal to teens: 'Sleep all day, party all night, never grow old, and never die. It's fun being a vampire.' Kiefer Sutherland featured as one of the main vampires, David.

INTERVIEW WITH THE VAMPIRE: THE VAMPIRE CHRONICLES (1994)

The film adaptations of Anne Rice's classic vampire books saw some drop-dead gorgeous actors in the leading roles. Lestat de Lioncourt was played by Tom Cruise, Christian Slater played Daniel Malloy and Louis de Pointe du Lac was played by Brad Pitt. Initially Anne Rice couldn't see Tom Cruise as Lestat, but he won her over with his performance.

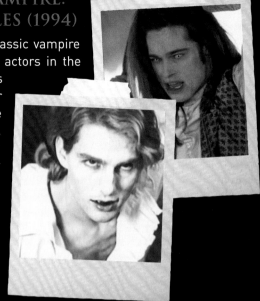

BUFFY THE VAMPIRE SLAYER (1997–2003)

This hit TV series and its spin-off, Angel, were the dominant vampire showcases of the nineties. Created by Joss Whedon, the show starred Sarah Michelle Gellar in the title role and David Boreanaz as one of the lead vampires, Angel. A vampire with a soul, Angel was Buffy's main love interest.

CIRQUE DU FREAK: THE VAMPIRE'S ASSISTANT (2009)

Another recent twist on vampire mythology, Darren Shan's vampires don't bite humans to drink their blood – and they don't kill them either! If they do kill a human, they become an evil, purple-skinned, red-eyed creature called a Vampaneze.

WHY VAMPIRES, WHY NOW?

Discover why some of your favourite actors, actresses and creators think vampires are so hot right now!

'A VAMPIRE CAN BE GOOD-LOOKING AND ALSO DANGEROUS. [IT'S] THE ONLY CHARACTER [THAT] CAN.'

– ROBERT PATTINSON, *TWILIGHT*

'I THINK THERE'S A SENSUALITY ABOUT VAMPIRES, A MONSTROUSNESS. THEY OFFER UP ETERNAL LIFE IN EXCHANGE FOR BLOOD. THERE'S SOMETHING INTENSE ABOUT WANTING SOMEONE SO MUCH THAT YOU HAVE TO DEVOUR THEM. THE BITING OF THE NECK, IT'S SEXY!'

– PETER FACINELLI, *TWILIGHT*

'I THINK EVERYBODY'S ALWAYS ATTRACTED TO THE VAMPIRE GENRE. I'VE ALWAYS BEEN MYSELF. AND THE MYTHOLOGY OF BEING IMMORTAL AND INVULNERABLE, BASICALLY, IT'S SOMETHING EXTREME. I'VE ALWAYS BEEN ATTRACTED TO EXTREMES IN LIFE AND IN STORIES AND ART. I THINK THAT'S WHY PEOPLE ARE HERE BECAUSE IT'S EXTREME, YET AT THE SAME TIME IT'S GROUNDED IN MORALITY.'

– JACKSON RATHBONE, *TWILIGHT*

'IT'S THE UNKNOWN. AND IT'S NOT JUST WITH VAMPIRES. WITH ANYTHING – A PERSON, A DESTINATION – THAT WE DON'T KNOW FOR SURE, WHERE MYSTERY SURROUNDS IT, THAT'S EXCITING. SO IT'S ATTRACTIVE. AND WITH VAMPIRES YOU HAVE THEIR SEXUALITY. IT'S LIKE THE BEST OF BOTH WORLDS. YOU HAVE THIS UNKNOWN WORLD AND YOU HAVE THIS RAW SEXUAL POWER, AND THE AMOUNT OF STRENGTH AND INTENSITY INVOLVED WHEN YOU COMBINE BOTH OF THOSE IS EXTREMELY CAPTIVATING. IT'S NOT JUST TWILIGHT. IT'S ALL OF THESE VAMPIRE THINGS THAT ARE OUT NOW.'

– CAM GIGANDET, *TWILIGHT*

True Blood creator Alan Ball.

'I THINK VAMPIRES ARE A TIMELESS, POWERFUL ARCHETYPE THAT CAN TAP INTO PEOPLE'S PSYCHES. THEY'VE BEEN AROUND FOREVER, EVEN BEFORE THE REINVENTION OF VAMPIRES IN THE 1990S WITH [FRANCIS FORD COPPOLA'S FILM] BRAM STOKER'S *DRACULA*. A LOT OF WORLD MYTHOLOGY ALL OVER THE GLOBE HAS CREATURES LIKE THE SUCCUBUS, THE ONE THAT FEEDS ON THE ESSENCE OF PEOPLE. I DON'T REALLY KNOW WHY THIS IS ALL HAPPENING AT THIS TIME, I'M JUST GLAD IT'S HAPPENING.'

– ALAN BALL, *TRUE BLOOD*

'FIRST OF ALL, SEX AND VIOLENCE ARE ALWAYS SOMETHING THAT ATTRACTS AN AUDIENCE, AND VAMPIRE STORIES USUALLY HAVE A LOT OF BOTH. AND, VAMPIRES SYMBOLIZE CONSISTENCY AND SOMETHING THAT'S PERMANENT IN A WORLD WHERE EVERYTHING IS CONSTANTLY CHANGING – HUMANS, ANIMALS, NATURE AND EVEN MOUNTAINS WILL CHANGE OVER TIME. TO HAVE SOMETHING THAT WILL JUST STAND THE TEST OF TIME IS ATTRACTIVE.'

– ALEXANDER SKARSGÅRD, *TRUE BLOOD*

'I THINK WHAT PEOPLE FAIL TO REALIZE IS THAT WITHIN THIS VAMPIRE GENRE THERE'S AN IMMENSE AMOUNT OF STORY-TELLING CAPABILITY. THERE ARE A LOT OF GREAT STORIES THAT COME OUT OF THIS. THAT'S WHY IT'S SO POPULAR.'

– IAN SOMERHALDER, *THE VAMPIRE DIARIES*

'I'VE GOT TO SAY, THAT THE VAMPIRE THING – IT'S THE WISH FULFILLMENT. EVERY WOMAN WANTS TO BE TAKEN BY A DANGEROUS, YET PURE-OF-HEART VAMPIRE.'

– JULIE PEC, *THE VAMPIRE DIARIES*

COMING UP...

Want to know where your next vampire fix is coming from? Apart from the tantalising wait for *Breaking Dawn* (2011 and 2012), along with new seasons of *True Blood* and *The Vampire Diaries*, some really exciting bloodsucking projects are in the pipeline... It's up to you to determine who'll become the next vampire superstar!

DARK SHADOWS

Immensely popular in its day, *Dark Shadows* was a 1960s gothic soap about Barnabas Collins, a 175-year-old vampire from Collinsport, Maine. *Alice in Wonderland* director Tim Burton said that he would love to bring Barnabas to the screen soon. And who is to be his leading man? None other than his longtime collaborator, Johnny Depp. Playing Barnabas has been 'a lifelong dream for me,' said Depp. 'I was obsessed with Barnabas Collins. I have photographs of me holding Barnabas Collins posters when I was five or six.' Depp may well rival Robert Pattinson as the sexiest vampire yet!

THE HISTORIAN

Most successful vampire franchises have been adapted from a best-selling book or series and as recent vampire fiction goes, one of the most successful is Elizabeth Kostova's *The Historian*. Central to the tale is Vlad the Impaler (often cited as the main inspiration for Dracula), but this movie has been 'in production' for two years already, so it may be some time before we get to see it on the big screen.

ACKNOWLEDGEMENTS

Many thanks to the whole John Blake Publishing team and to Sophie,
who secretly is a vampire – this book is for you!

Published by John Blake Publishing Ltd,
3 Bramber Court, 2 Bramber Road,
London W14 9PB, England

www.johnblakepublishing.co.uk

First published in hardback in 2010

ISBN: 978 1 84358 264 9

British Library Cataloguing-in-Publication Data:

A catalogue record for this book is available from the British Library.

Design by www.envydesign.co.uk

Printed in Barcelona, Spain, by Indice SL

1 3 5 7 9 10 8 6 4 2

All pictures courtesy of Wenn Images, except page 7 (top), 15 (middle & bottom), 26, 28,
30, 32, 33, 38, 40, 44, 45, 50, 56 (t & m), 57 (t & m), 61, and the following which are
courtesy of Rex Features: page 13, 24 (b), 31, 42, 47, 48 (t), 56 (b)

Papers used by John Blake Publishing are natural, recyclable products made
from wood grown in sustainable forests. The manufacturing processes conform
to the environmental regulations of the country of origin.

Every attempt has been made to contact the relevant copyright-holders, but
some were unobtainable. We would be grateful if the appropriate people
could contact us.